As you document

first year of your

live each day min

journal serve as a precious keepsake for many

generations to come.

OUR MOST PRECIOUS MOMENTS WITH:

_____

YEAR:

_____

DATE & AGE:

sweet moments

_____
_____
_____
_____
_____
_____
_____
_____
_____
_____

DATE & AGE:

you touched my heart

_____
_____
_____
_____
_____
_____
_____
_____
_____

DATE & AGE: [_____]

my smiles for today

_____
_____
_____
_____
_____
_____
_____
_____
_____
_____

DATE & AGE: [_____]

I will never forget

_____
_____
_____
_____
_____
_____
_____
_____
_____
_____

DATE & AGE: [   ]

best moments

_____

_____

_____

_____

_____

_____

_____

_____

_____

DATE & AGE: [   ]

memories made

_____

_____

_____

_____

_____

_____

_____

_____

_____

DATE & AGE: [   ]

today was remarkable

_____
_____
_____
_____
_____
_____
_____
_____
_____

DATE & AGE: [   ]

remember these moments

_____
_____
_____
_____
_____
_____
_____
_____
_____

DATE & AGE: [   ]

sweet moments

_____
_____
_____
_____
_____
_____
_____
_____
_____

DATE & AGE: [   ]

you touched my heart

_____
_____
_____
_____
_____
_____
_____
_____
_____

DATE & AGE:

my smiles for today

_____

_____

_____

_____

_____

_____

_____

_____

_____

_____

DATE & AGE:

I will never forget

_____

_____

_____

_____

_____

_____

_____

_____

_____

_____

DATE & AGE:

best moments

_____

_____

_____

_____

_____

_____

_____

_____

_____

DATE & AGE:

memories made

_____

_____

_____

_____

_____

_____

_____

_____

_____

DATE & AGE:

today was remarkable

_____

_____

_____

_____

_____

_____

_____

_____

_____

DATE & AGE:

remember these moments

_____

_____

_____

_____

_____

_____

_____

_____

_____

DATE & AGE: [   ]

sweet moments

_____
_____
_____
_____
_____
_____
_____
_____
_____
_____

DATE & AGE: [   ]

you touched my heart

_____
_____
_____
_____
_____
_____
_____
_____
_____

DATE & AGE:

my smiles for today

_____

_____

_____

_____

_____

_____

_____

_____

_____

_____

DATE & AGE:

I will never forget

_____

_____

_____

_____

_____

_____

_____

_____

_____

_____

DATE & AGE: [   ]

best moments

_____
_____
_____
_____
_____
_____
_____
_____
_____

DATE & AGE: [   ]

memories made

_____
_____
_____
_____
_____
_____
_____
_____
_____

DATE & AGE:

today was remarkable

_____
_____
_____
_____
_____
_____
_____
_____
_____
_____

DATE & AGE:

remember these moments

_____
_____
_____
_____
_____
_____
_____
_____
_____
_____

DATE & AGE: [   ]

sweet moments

_____

_____

_____

_____

_____

_____

_____

_____

_____

_____

DATE & AGE: [   ]

you touched my heart

_____

_____

_____

_____

_____

_____

_____

_____

_____

_____

DATE & AGE:

my smiles for today

_____

_____

_____

_____

_____

_____

_____

_____

_____

_____

DATE & AGE:

I will never forget

_____

_____

_____

_____

_____

_____

_____

_____

_____

_____

DATE & AGE:

best moments

_____

_____

_____

_____

_____

_____

_____

_____

_____

DATE & AGE:

memories made

_____

_____

_____

_____

_____

_____

_____

_____

_____

DATE & AGE:

today was remarkable

_____

_____

_____

_____

_____

_____

_____

_____

_____

DATE & AGE:

remember these moments

_____

_____

_____

_____

_____

_____

_____

_____

_____

DATE & AGE:

sweet moments

_____
_____
_____
_____
_____
_____
_____
_____
_____

DATE & AGE:

you touched my heart

_____
_____
_____
_____
_____
_____
_____
_____
_____

DATE & AGE:

my smiles for today

_____

_____

_____

_____

_____

_____

_____

_____

_____

DATE & AGE:

I will never forget

_____

_____

_____

_____

_____

_____

_____

_____

_____

DATE & AGE:

best moments

_____
_____
_____
_____
_____
_____
_____
_____
_____

DATE & AGE:

memories made

_____
_____
_____
_____
_____
_____
_____
_____
_____

DATE & AGE:

today was remarkable

_____
_____
_____
_____
_____
_____
_____
_____
_____
_____

DATE & AGE:

remember these moments

_____
_____
_____
_____
_____
_____
_____
_____
_____
_____

DATE & AGE: [   ]

sweet moments

_____
_____
_____
_____
_____
_____
_____
_____
_____

DATE & AGE: [   ]

you touched my heart

_____
_____
_____
_____
_____
_____
_____
_____
_____

DATE & AGE:

my smiles for today

_____

_____

_____

_____

_____

_____

_____

_____

_____

_____

DATE & AGE:

I will never forget

_____

_____

_____

_____

_____

_____

_____

_____

_____

_____

DATE & AGE:

best moments

_____
_____
_____
_____
_____
_____
_____
_____
_____

DATE & AGE:

memories made

_____
_____
_____
_____
_____
_____
_____
_____
_____

DATE & AGE:

today was remarkable

_____

_____

_____

_____

_____

_____

_____

_____

_____

DATE & AGE:

remember these moments

_____

_____

_____

_____

_____

_____

_____

_____

_____

DATE & AGE:

sweet moments

_____
_____
_____
_____
_____
_____
_____
_____

DATE & AGE:

you touched my heart

_____
_____
_____
_____
_____
_____
_____
_____
_____

DATE & AGE:

my smiles for today

_____
_____
_____
_____
_____
_____
_____
_____
_____
_____

DATE & AGE:

I will never forget

_____
_____
_____
_____
_____
_____
_____
_____
_____
_____

DATE & AGE:

best moments

_____
_____
_____
_____
_____
_____
_____
_____
_____

DATE & AGE:

memories made

_____
_____
_____
_____
_____
_____
_____
_____

DATE & AGE:

today was remarkable

_____

_____

_____

_____

_____

_____

_____

_____

_____

DATE & AGE:

remember these moments

_____

_____

_____

_____

_____

_____

_____

_____

_____

DATE & AGE:

sweet moments

_____

_____

_____

_____

_____

_____

_____

_____

_____

DATE & AGE:

you touched my heart

_____

_____

_____

_____

_____

_____

_____

_____

_____

DATE & AGE:

my smiles for today

_____

_____

_____

_____

_____

_____

_____

_____

_____

_____

DATE & AGE:

I will never forget

_____

_____

_____

_____

_____

_____

_____

_____

_____

_____

DATE & AGE:

best moments

_____

_____

_____

_____

_____

_____

_____

_____

_____

DATE & AGE:

memories made

_____

_____

_____

_____

_____

_____

_____

_____

_____

DATE & AGE:

today was remarkable

_____
_____
_____
_____
_____
_____
_____
_____
_____
_____

DATE & AGE:

remember these moments

_____
_____
_____
_____
_____
_____
_____
_____
_____
_____

DATE & AGE:

sweet moments

_____

_____

_____

_____

_____

_____

_____

_____

_____

_____

DATE & AGE:

you touched my heart

_____

_____

_____

_____

_____

_____

_____

_____

_____

_____

DATE & AGE:

my smiles for today

_____

_____

_____

_____

_____

_____

_____

_____

_____

_____

DATE & AGE:

I will never forget

_____

_____

_____

_____

_____

_____

_____

_____

_____

_____

DATE & AGE:

best moments

_____
_____
_____
_____
_____
_____
_____
_____
_____

DATE & AGE:

memories made

_____
_____
_____
_____
_____
_____
_____
_____
_____

DATE & AGE:

today was remarkable

_____
_____
_____
_____
_____
_____
_____
_____
_____
_____

DATE & AGE:

remember these moments

_____
_____
_____
_____
_____
_____
_____
_____
_____
_____

DATE & AGE:

sweet moments

_____

_____

_____

_____

_____

_____

_____

_____

_____

DATE & AGE:

you touched my heart

_____

_____

_____

_____

_____

_____

_____

_____

DATE & AGE: [   ]

my smiles for today

_____

_____

_____

_____

_____

_____

_____

_____

_____

DATE & AGE: [   ]

I will never forget

_____

_____

_____

_____

_____

_____

_____

_____

_____

DATE & AGE:

best moments

_____
_____
_____
_____
_____
_____
_____
_____
_____

DATE & AGE:

memories made

_____
_____
_____
_____
_____
_____
_____
_____
_____

DATE & AGE:

today was remarkable

_____

_____

_____

_____

_____

_____

_____

_____

_____

DATE & AGE:

remember these moments

_____

_____

_____

_____

_____

_____

_____

_____

_____

DATE & AGE:

sweet moments

_____

_____

_____

_____

_____

_____

_____

_____

DATE & AGE:

you touched my heart

_____

_____

_____

_____

_____

_____

_____

_____

DATE & AGE:

my smiles for today

_____

_____

_____

_____

_____

_____

_____

_____

_____

_____

DATE & AGE:

I will never forget

_____

_____

_____

_____

_____

_____

_____

_____

_____

_____

DATE & AGE:

best moments

_____
_____
_____
_____
_____
_____
_____
_____
_____

DATE & AGE:

memories made

_____
_____
_____
_____
_____
_____
_____
_____
_____

DATE & AGE:

today was remarkable

_____

_____

_____

_____

_____

_____

_____

_____

_____

_____

DATE & AGE:

remember these moments

_____

_____

_____

_____

_____

_____

_____

_____

_____

_____

DATE & AGE:

sweet moments

_____

_____

_____

_____

_____

_____

_____

_____

_____

DATE & AGE:

you touched my heart

_____

_____

_____

_____

_____

_____

_____

_____

_____

DATE & AGE:

my smiles for today

_____

_____

_____

_____

_____

_____

_____

_____

_____

_____

DATE & AGE:

I will never forget

_____

_____

_____

_____

_____

_____

_____

_____

_____

DATE & AGE:

best moments

_____
_____
_____
_____
_____
_____
_____
_____
_____

DATE & AGE:

memories made

_____
_____
_____
_____
_____
_____
_____
_____
_____

DATE & AGE:

today was remarkable

_____
_____
_____
_____
_____
_____
_____
_____
_____
_____

DATE & AGE:

remember these moments

_____
_____
_____
_____
_____
_____
_____
_____
_____
_____

DATE & AGE:

sweet moments

_____

_____

_____

_____

_____

_____

_____

_____

_____

DATE & AGE:

you touched my heart

_____

_____

_____

_____

_____

_____

_____

_____

_____

DATE & AGE:

my smiles for today

_____

_____

_____

_____

_____

_____

_____

_____

_____

_____

DATE & AGE:

I will never forget

_____

_____

_____

_____

_____

_____

_____

_____

_____

_____

DATE & AGE:

best moments

_____
_____
_____
_____
_____
_____
_____
_____
_____

DATE & AGE:

memories made

_____
_____
_____
_____
_____
_____
_____
_____
_____

DATE & AGE:

today was remarkable

_____

_____

_____

_____

_____

_____

_____

_____

_____

_____

DATE & AGE:

remember these moments

_____

_____

_____

_____

_____

_____

_____

_____

_____

_____

DATE & AGE:

sweet moments

_____

_____

_____

_____

_____

_____

_____

_____

_____

DATE & AGE:

you touched my heart

_____

_____

_____

_____

_____

_____

_____

_____

_____

DATE & AGE:

my smiles for today

_____

_____

_____

_____

_____

_____

_____

_____

_____

_____

DATE & AGE:

I will never forget

_____

_____

_____

_____

_____

_____

_____

_____

_____

_____

DATE & AGE: [   ]

best moments

_____
_____
_____
_____
_____
_____
_____
_____
_____

DATE & AGE: [   ]

memories made

_____
_____
_____
_____
_____
_____
_____
_____
_____

DATE & AGE:

today was remarkable

_____

_____

_____

_____

_____

_____

_____

_____

_____

_____

DATE & AGE:

remember these moments

_____

_____

_____

_____

_____

_____

_____

_____

_____

_____

DATE & AGE:

sweet moments

_____

_____

_____

_____

_____

_____

_____

_____

_____

DATE & AGE:

you touched my heart

_____

_____

_____

_____

_____

_____

_____

_____

_____

DATE & AGE:

my smiles for today

_____

_____

_____

_____

_____

_____

_____

_____

_____

_____

DATE & AGE:

I will never forget

_____

_____

_____

_____

_____

_____

_____

_____

_____

_____

DATE & AGE:

best moments

_____
_____
_____
_____
_____
_____
_____
_____

DATE & AGE:

memories made

_____
_____
_____
_____
_____
_____
_____
_____

DATE & AGE:

today was remarkable

_____

_____

_____

_____

_____

_____

_____

_____

_____

_____

DATE & AGE:

remember these moments

_____

_____

_____

_____

_____

_____

_____

_____

_____

_____

DATE & AGE:

sweet moments

_____

_____

_____

_____

_____

_____

_____

_____

_____

DATE & AGE:

you touched my heart

_____

_____

_____

_____

_____

_____

_____

_____

_____

DATE & AGE:

my smiles for today

_____

_____

_____

_____

_____

_____

_____

_____

_____

_____

DATE & AGE:

I will never forget

_____

_____

_____

_____

_____

_____

_____

_____

_____

_____

DATE & AGE:

best moments

_____
_____
_____
_____
_____
_____
_____
_____
_____

DATE & AGE:

memories made

_____
_____
_____
_____
_____
_____
_____
_____
_____

DATE & AGE:

today was remarkable

_____

_____

_____

_____

_____

_____

_____

_____

_____

DATE & AGE:

remember these moments

_____

_____

_____

_____

_____

_____

_____

_____

_____

DATE & AGE:

sweet moments

_____

_____

_____

_____

_____

_____

_____

_____

_____

DATE & AGE:

you touched my heart

_____

_____

_____

_____

_____

_____

_____

_____

_____

DATE & AGE:

my smiles for today

_____

_____

_____

_____

_____

_____

_____

_____

_____

DATE & AGE:

I will never forget

_____

_____

_____

_____

_____

_____

_____

_____

_____

DATE & AGE:

best moments

_____

_____

_____

_____

_____

_____

_____

_____

DATE & AGE:

memories made

_____

_____

_____

_____

_____

_____

_____

_____

DATE & AGE:

today was remarkable

_____

_____

_____

_____

_____

_____

_____

_____

_____

DATE & AGE:

remember these moments

_____

_____

_____

_____

_____

_____

_____

_____

_____

DATE & AGE:

sweet moments

_____

_____

_____

_____

_____

_____

_____

_____

DATE & AGE:

you touched my heart

_____

_____

_____

_____

_____

_____

_____

_____

_____

DATE & AGE:

my smiles for today

_____

_____

_____

_____

_____

_____

_____

_____

_____

_____

DATE & AGE:

I will never forget

_____

_____

_____

_____

_____

_____

_____

_____

_____

_____

DATE & AGE:

best moments

_____

_____

_____

_____

_____

_____

_____

_____

DATE & AGE:

memories made

_____

_____

_____

_____

_____

_____

_____

_____

DATE & AGE:

today was remarkable

_____

_____

_____

_____

_____

_____

_____

_____

_____

DATE & AGE:

remember these moments

_____

_____

_____

_____

_____

_____

_____

_____

_____

DATE & AGE: [   ]

sweet moments

_____

_____

_____

_____

_____

_____

_____

_____

_____

DATE & AGE: [   ]

you touched my heart

_____

_____

_____

_____

_____

_____

_____

_____

_____

DATE & AGE: [_____]

my smiles for today

_____

_____

_____

_____

_____

_____

_____

_____

_____

_____

DATE & AGE: [_____]

I will never forget

_____

_____

_____

_____

_____

_____

_____

_____

_____

_____

DATE & AGE:

best moments

_____
_____
_____
_____
_____
_____
_____
_____
_____

DATE & AGE:

memories made

_____
_____
_____
_____
_____
_____
_____
_____
_____

DATE & AGE:

today was remarkable

_____

_____

_____

_____

_____

_____

_____

_____

_____

DATE & AGE:

remember these moments

_____

_____

_____

_____

_____

_____

_____

_____

_____

DATE & AGE:

sweet moments

_____

_____

_____

_____

_____

_____

_____

_____

DATE & AGE:

you touched my heart

_____

_____

_____

_____

_____

_____

_____

_____

_____

DATE & AGE:

my smiles for today

_____

_____

_____

_____

_____

_____

_____

_____

_____

_____

DATE & AGE:

I will never forget

_____

_____

_____

_____

_____

_____

_____

_____

_____

_____

DATE & AGE:

best moments

_____

_____

_____

_____

_____

_____

_____

_____

_____

DATE & AGE:

memories made

_____

_____

_____

_____

_____

_____

_____

_____

_____

DATE & AGE:

today was remarkable

_____

_____

_____

_____

_____

_____

_____

_____

_____

DATE & AGE:

remember these moments

_____

_____

_____

_____

_____

_____

_____

_____

_____

DATE & AGE:

sweet moments

_____
_____
_____
_____
_____
_____
_____
_____
_____

DATE & AGE:

you touched my heart

_____
_____
_____
_____
_____
_____
_____
_____
_____

DATE & AGE:

my smiles for today

_____

_____

_____

_____

_____

_____

_____

_____

DATE & AGE:

I will never forget

_____

_____

_____

_____

_____

_____

_____

_____

DATE & AGE:

best moments

_____

_____

_____

_____

_____

_____

_____

_____

_____

DATE & AGE:

memories made

_____

_____

_____

_____

_____

_____

_____

_____

_____

DATE & AGE: [   ]

today was remarkable

_____
_____
_____
_____
_____
_____
_____
_____
_____
_____

DATE & AGE: [   ]

remember these moments

_____
_____
_____
_____
_____
_____
_____
_____
_____
_____

DATE & AGE:

sweet moments

_____
_____
_____
_____
_____
_____
_____
_____

DATE & AGE:

you touched my heart

_____
_____
_____
_____
_____
_____
_____
_____

DATE & AGE:

my smiles for today

_____

_____

_____

_____

_____

_____

_____

_____

_____

DATE & AGE:

I will never forget

_____

_____

_____

_____

_____

_____

_____

_____

_____

DATE & AGE:

best moments

_____

_____

_____

_____

_____

_____

_____

_____

_____

DATE & AGE:

memories made

_____

_____

_____

_____

_____

_____

_____

_____

_____

DATE & AGE: [ ]

today was remarkable

_____
_____
_____
_____
_____
_____
_____
_____
_____

DATE & AGE: [ ]

remember these moments

_____
_____
_____
_____
_____
_____
_____
_____
_____

DATE & AGE:

sweet moments

_____
_____
_____
_____
_____
_____
_____
_____

DATE & AGE:

you touched my heart

_____
_____
_____
_____
_____
_____
_____
_____
_____

DATE & AGE:

my smiles for today

_____

_____

_____

_____

_____

_____

_____

_____

_____

DATE & AGE:

I will never forget

_____

_____

_____

_____

_____

_____

_____

_____

_____

DATE & AGE:

best moments

_____
_____
_____
_____
_____
_____
_____
_____
_____
_____

DATE & AGE:

memories made

_____
_____
_____
_____
_____
_____
_____
_____
_____

DATE & AGE:

today was remarkable

_____

_____

_____

_____

_____

_____

_____

_____

_____

DATE & AGE:

remember these moments

_____

_____

_____

_____

_____

_____

_____

_____

_____

Made in United States
Troutdale, OR
04/24/2025

30878327R00080